How to E
A Successful
Programmer
Without a Degree

Eric Frick

Published By Eric Frick 2017

Copyright

Contents

Forward

Welcome to Become a Successful Programmer without a Degree, where I will take you through the process needed to be completed to become a successful programmer. My name is Eric Frick and I have worked in the IT industry for over 30 years. In addition to working as an IT Instructor, I have worked as a senior IT manager in several different organizations. I have interviewed hundreds of programmers and I know what IT managers are looking for in a strong candidate.

With the shortage of programmers today and the high salaries that programmers command, many people are looking for a career change and a way to get into this exciting field. This book is designed to help you develop a plan of action to do just that. I will take you through step by step in how to develop your plan and have provided examples that can help you along the way. This plan will give you a real idea of the time and commitment it will take you to become a programmer.

In this book, I will first take you through the concepts you need to master in order to become a programmer. Next, I will take you through the equipment you will need and the training classes you need to complete. Following that, I will outline some tips on writing up your resume, tips in looking for a job and some interview tips.

This course is designed for students who want to become a full-time programmer. It is also ideal for someone who is contemplating a career change and wants to know how they can complete a program of study that is outside of traditional university program. By the end of this book, you will have your own complete plan of study. So if you are thinking about becoming a programmer this is a great first step – develop a plan!

Thank you for your interest in this book! Undertaking this training will not be easy, but it can lead to a financially rewarding and interesting career. In the next chapters, I will lay out all of the items you need to consider when developing your plan.

Why Become a Programmer?

In this first chapter,I will talk about some of the motivation of why you want to become a programmer?   I will talk briefly about some of the motivating factors for becoming a programmer. I will also talk about some of the elements that make being a programmer or software developer a good career move. Then I will lay out the structure of the rest of this book.

Becoming a programmer can be an excellent job choice. I have been involved with software development for over 30 years and have really enjoyed the software development aspects of my career. I want to share with you some of my experiences of my career and also some of those things that will help you become very successful.

Software development jobs pay very well. I have included a reference that states that the average salary for a software developer is over $95,000. This figure is from an article I found online from US news.

It should noted that this figure is for the United States and salaries are very dependent on what part of the world you work in. Many of my students work in countries outside the United States so I wanted to make sure to be clear that this figure is only for the United States. Another great factor for becoming a software developer is the job demand continues to remain strong. Other things can change, but I do not see this changing in the near future. The demand for software and computer products continues to rise. In addition to being a good paying job, there is also a potential entry into IT management which pays significantly higher. All of these factors make becoming a programmer a very sensible job choice. Now that we have talked about this a little bit let's talk about the remainder of this book.

In the first part of this book, I will go over some of the basic skills that you will need to master to become a software developer. I will also talk about how to select a programming language that you would like to gain expertise in. I will also talk about the equipment that you will need to practice your materials to become a software developer. In the last part of this section, I will talk about some of the computer science concepts that you will need to master to become an entry-level developer. These concepts will drive the training plan that is necessary for you to develop the skills to master these concepts.

In part two of this book, I will talk about some of the items you need to help you in developing your training plan. I will talk about the types of training that are available today and some of the advantages and disadvantages of each of those types of training methods. I will also talk about how to get some experience so you have some projects and references you can list on your resume. In the last part of this section, I will show you how to put together a master plan and budget to pull all of this together. I have included some master plans and examples that you can download and modify for your own plan.

In the last part of this book, I will talk about how to go about getting your first job. I will talk about some places to go search for jobs and some options to help find leads for jobs. I will also talk about how to prepare your resume. I have included some sample resumes you might use to help you format your own resume. Next, I will talk about how to prepare for your job interview. I have also included some tips for your job interview that I have learned over my thirty-year career that can help you.

I have tried to include as many examples as I can over my career that will help you get started with your new career. I have literally interviewed hundreds of programmers during my career and I will give you some valuable tips that will help you know what hiring managers look for when they hire a new programmer. Do not underestimate what it takes to become a programmer there are a lot of skills to master and this will require time and dedication to master the necessary skills to become a successful programmer. But do not let that stop you on your quest to become a software developer. Writing software for a living is a very satisfying career alon with being financially rewarding.

So just a short word of encouragement you can do this! Time, dedication and perseverance will help you fulfill your goal.

Exercise 1 Write Down Your High-Level Goals

For this exercise, you will define your basic goals for your program. You should define the following:

- Basic Purpose
    - Why do you want to do this? What are your strengths?
    - Biggest Risk
    - What do you think your biggest hurdle will be? Time? Money? Something else?
- Timetable
    - Should not be longer than 24 months
- Basic Budget
    - Be realistic about what you can reasonably afford

I have included two sample sets of goals to give you some ideas of the types of things you might consider.

Sample Goals 1

- Purpose: I want to become a full-stack web developer and get a good paying regular job in Columbus, Ohio. I would like to make $65,000 per year starting out. I think I have a very good attention to detail and I like building things. I already have a fast computer that I think I can use to practice web development.
- Biggest Risk: I think my biggest risk is finding time to work on the coding exercises and making sure

my day job does not suffer or interfere. I have already begun to build out an office in my basement where I can study regularly. I have also asked my next door neighbor who works as a programmer at a local company to help me.

- Timetable: I would like to complete this program in 18 months:
- Basic Budget: I have saved about $3000 to invest in online training and books.

<u>Sample Goals 2</u>

- Purpose: I want to become a full-stack web developer and get a good paying regular job in Los Angeles, CA. I would like to make $85,000 per year starting.
- Biggest Risk: I think my biggest risk is devoting time for the 14 week boot camp program. I will not be able to work during that period and will have to live off my savings until I complete the program. I also need to check out the boot camp program with the local Better Business Bureau to make sure they do not have any pending complaints.
- Timetable: I would like to sign up for a local boot camp and complete the program in 6 months
- Basic Budget: I am planning on getting a loan to finance the $12,000 fee for the 14 week boot camp program.

What Skills Will I Need?

SKiLLS

In this chapter, I will describe the basic skills you need to become a successful programmer in today's market. You will need a number of skills in addition to good coding skills in order to become a valued member of a software development team. Once you have landed your first job, you will find that much of your day is spent in team meetings with the development team and meetings. These meetings are with the customers to help define requirements and then testing your product. To be a complete member of the team you will need the following skills:

- Communication
- Problem solving
- Anticipate customer needs
- Persistence
- Ability to adapt to change, and
- Good coding skills

Communication

Programming is a "Team" sport. Working within a team is a critical factor to success in your career. Many of the projects involve large teams of people which makes communications more difficult. To assist with this communication, you will need to be able to quickly and effectively report bugs and issues to the project management. In addition, you will need to be able to interact with customers to help fix any bugs that are found in the system.

Work on most projects is completed off of formal written specifications. Because of this, you will need to be able to interpret these specifications and turn them into working code. Many times there are questions and issues that need to be resolved with the customers before they can be coded. You will need to be able to quickly resolve these questions with customers in order to keep your project on time and within budget.

Development efforts are expensive and time-consuming efforts. In order to keep these projects on track you may be asked to help prepare progress reports. These reports are usually prepared weekly and are used to help find potential problems and resolve them quickly and effectively. To help prepare these reports you will need to be able to write up project details from a development perspective and communicate these to the project management team.

Many software systems are critical to a company's daily operations. Because of this, fixing bugs and issues often become very high priority items for programmers working on these systems. Because of the critical nature of some of these systems, you may find that you are working with high levels of management within the company. This level of management wants a very quick and complete update on the status of these systems. You will need to be able to juggle multiple priorities and quickly and effectively communicate the status to the management team. This becomes even more challenging if one of these mission critical systems is down for any length of time.

These are just some of the examples of the communication demands that can be placed on programmers that are part of a development team. As you rise in the ranks of the development team these demands on you will increase over time. So do not overlook the importance of having good communication skills.

Problem Solving

Another skill you will need is the ability to solve complex problems. IT projects are often large and complex. Supporting and fixing these systems will require you to help fix difficult problems. If these problems happen to the production system, you will have to troubleshoot and fix problems on the fly. Time may be at a premium if the problem you are trying to fix is causing a service outage. These problems may also be project related problems such as the project being behind schedule or over budget. Unfortunately, many of these problems may happen at difficult times and may require you to work on weekends or holidays. You should be prepared that becoming a software developer will require you to work long hours at certain times of a project. That may be the downside, but generally, developers are well compensated for their time.

Anticipate Customer Needs

All software development projects have customers, even if they are internal to a company. Anticipating customer needs by the development team is critical to a project success. Many times development efforts are funded by customers so keeping them happy will be necessary to keep the project funding in place. Many times customers have difficulty in defining software requirements since they are generally non-technical personnel and do not have software development experience. In addition, customer needs will change over time so they will need assistance from the development team in order to be successful. Delivering great customer service is important to your career!

Persistence

Fixing problems in complex software systems can be a long and frustrating process. Because of this, you will need the ability to be persistent and look at all problems from many different angles. In most cases, difficult problems are assigned to the most senior developer on the project due to the problem-solving problems that he/she have learned over time. In some cases, problems may need multiple approaches to solve particularly difficult issues. Developers who can consistently fix complex problems are rewarded!

Ability to Adapt to Change

The change in the IT and software development business is constant and rapid and therefore requires you to be able to adapt to change. Customer needs will change over time and your software will need to be able to adapt to that change. If you are working on a software product, you will need to be able to adapt to a changing market. Software companies that are not able to adapt to change will find themselves quickly out of business.

In addition, software development tools and techniques are constantly evolving. You will need to update your development skills over time to reflect these changes. Successful developers need to be able to embrace a lifetime of learning and continuing education. Fortunately, once you learn one programming language, learning another one is an easier process.

Good Coding Skills

Last but not least you will need good coding skills. Programmers need the ability to turn requirements and ideas into working code. This will require you to have a good command of a selected programming language. In addition, you will need to be able to turn out code efficiently enough to meet the demands of project schedules and budgets. This may require you to work extra hours in order to meet project deadlines. It is not uncommon for software development teams to work long hours as release dates are coming near.

In addition to writing code, you must also be able to master the use of a number of software development tools. The primary tool you must master is the use of a debugger from within your development environment. The debugger allows programmers to ensure that programs are functioning properly and efficiently.

Computer programs are complex pieces of logic. Your code must be understood by other programmers who will maintain your code over time. This means your code must be well structured and documented. In addition, you may be asked to participate in code reviews. This is where a team of programmers routinely reviews code as a group to help ensure all quality standards for the project are met. Other programmers will review your code for logic and completeness. They may also suggest alternate methods to improve the code. This process takes some time to become comfortable with and is often difficult for those programmers that have never participated in a code review.

In summary, becoming a successful programmer requires mastering a number of skills. When first starting out most people assume that writing code will be the only skill that is needed. Software development is a team activity and communicating and interacting with the team is critical to the success of your team and also the success of your career as a developer.

Java .NET or Something Else?

In this chapter I will talk about selecting your first programming language to learn. So let's go ahead and get started.

When you first start programming you should focus your development efforts on a single programming language. Once you become accomplished in one programming language it is much simpler to learn a new language after this. Some of the most common platforms on the market today are the Microsoft .NET platform, Java from Oracle, and the LAMP platform. I refer to these as platforms since in many cases they are more than just a programming language. There are also some other platforms that are becoming popular today and I will talk about those in a little bit more detail later. Let's go through each one of these platforms in more detail.

.NET

One of the most popular platforms is .NET from Microsoft. It is based on the .NET framework it is used primarily for developing applications for the Windows operating system. Although recently Microsoft has developed a version of the .NET framework for cross-platform development, it is still used primarily for Windows-based development. One of the unique things about .NET is that it supports multiple programming languages such as C#, Visual Basic, F# and others. C# is very similar to Java. It is one of the most popular languages supported by .NET. ASP .NET is the language used for web development. .NET can also be used to develop desktop applications, service development through WCF and mobile applications. Microsoft has recently added much more support for mobile application development through some key acquisitions, such as Xamarin.

Java

Another popular platform on the market today is Java. It was originally developed by Sun Microsystems which was was purchased by Oracle in 2010. Oracle now maintains and distributes Java products. It is based on the Java virtual machine or JVM. One of the unique things about Java is that it can run on multiple operating systems. This means you can develop software for Windows machines, Linux machines, or the iOS operating system. Java can be used for web development through Java server pages. It can also be used to develop desktop applications, enterprise applications, and mobile applications through the use of Android Studio.

LAMP

The next platform we will talk about is the LAMP platform. LAMP tools target software for the Linux operating system. LAMP utilizes the Apache Web server, the MySQL database, and the PHP programming environment. All of these are free tools and can be downloaded from the Internet. You can purchase support contracts from commercial companies to help you run and maintain these environments. This software is very popular in university environments, nonprofit organizations, government organizations and also some commercial applications. The free licensing costs are very attractive for many organizations who choose to implement the software.

Other Platforms

There are also many other platforms out on the market today. These include languages such as Drupal, older legacy languages such as COBOL and new cloud-based platforms such as Salesforce and Microsoft dynamics. However, the languages I covered earlier constitute the majority of the software development market currently. Software languages and techniques are constantly changing and you should be prepared to take advantage of new opportunities as they come about. Successful programmers engage as lifelong learners so you should be aware that if you pursue a career as a programmer you will constantly be required to learn new languages and techniques as they change.

So with all of this information how can I choose a development language? First, you should review vendor information on the programming languages I have described. You should see if any of the information there appeals to you and is something you might like to pursue. Next, you should look at the local job listings to see the types of programmers demanded in your area. You can also talk to some local staffing agencies to get their recommendations to see what companies are hiring with a particular language. You can also check with some of your friends and family to see what languages they are using at their workplace. Finally, you can check with local universities to see what languages they teach; this also might be a good clue as to what languages are in demand in the local area.

In summary, learning your first programming language will be highly useful in getting your first job. However, after that, things may change after you are employed. Technology is constantly changing and there will be opportunities to learn new technologies as they are rolled out. You should be prepared to take advantage of these new technology projects as they often lead to higher pay and possibly promotions. Do not worry because learning a second programming language it is far easier after you have learned your first programming language. Remember this is an industry that changes very quickly and you should expect change! This concludes this chapter I hope it has given you some good thoughts on which programming language to choose for your initial training.

What Investment Will I Need?

In this chapter, I will talk about the types of investments that you will need to be able to complete a program that will give you the sufficient background to become a successful programmer. You will need to be able to make an investment in three key areas. These are in investment in time, support, and also a financial investment. The first area to look at is an investment in time. You will need a substantial amount of time and commitment to be able to complete all the training necessary to become a programmer. The next area you will need support from your friends and family to be up to make this happen. Do not overlook this area as this will be important since you will need a substantial time commitment and self-discipline to be able to complete the training. The last area is in terms of a financial investment. You will need to invest some amount of money to be able to purchase the necessary equipment, purchase some books, and also some online training or invest in a programming boot camp. It is not possible to complete this training with zero dollar investment. You can, however, minimize the amount of money that you need to invest in the training, but thinking that you can complete a program of this complexity without any financial investment is not realistic. Now I will drill down to each of these areas in a little bit more detail.

Time

The first area is the investment in time. The majority of your time will be spent studying materials and practicing coding. This area will require a lot of self-discipline and it will really help you to have a regularly scheduled time and place that you can work on your programming skills. It will be ideal if you can have an office or a study area where you live that can be a dedicated space that will be quiet and a great place to regularly work on your training materials. In terms of time, it is better to schedule a regular time to work on materials so it looks like a standard class. It's easy to let other priorities drive your schedule and fall behind on your training. Try to keep your end goals in mind as you are studying each day to prepare for your new career.

Support

Support is one area I think that many aspiring programmers often overlook. Going back to school in a traditional program, you will need your friends and family to help encourage and support you as you proceed throughout your training. It would be ideal to find a mentor or somebody who is already working as a programmer that can help you. You might also reach out to find a local programming group that you might join so that you can begin networking with people already working in the industry. You will find the people already working in the industry often times will be willing to help you.

Financial Investment

The next area I will talk about the is financial investment you will need to make in order to become a programmer. I have had many of my students over the years believe that they can do this just by looking at materials over the Internet and not make a financial investment. I have not known anyone that has been able to accomplish this without at least a minimal investment in money.   First and foremost you will need a very good computing environment to develop code. We will talk about this in a later chapter and I will show you some alternatives that can lower the cost you will need to invest in equipment. Unfortunately, to develop code you will need a very fast computer. Using an older computer with the slower processor only leads to frustration. I will include some additional estimates of costs in the planning section of this book.

In summary, you need to be realistic with yourself on what you can commit to in terms of time and money to complete your training. You will develop a plan and the timetable in an exercise later in this book. You will be able to write down all of the details you will need to complete your plan. Once you develop your plan you need to stick to the plan and work diligently to make it happen. Again to encourage you, think about your end goals for motivation. This is a growing field with very high-paying jobs that will allow you an opportunity for an excellent career. Stick to it you can do it!

What Equipment Will I Need?

In this lesson, I will talk about the type of equipment that you will need to develop code and train on.

In terms of the equipment that you will need, the first thing is a computer. You will need to decide what is best for you a desktop computer or a laptop. A laptop has an advantage that is, it is a mobile device and which means you can really develop anywhere, but a desktop device is generally faster it will allow you a better long-term environment for writing code. You can also use a hybrid environment by using a fast notebook computer and then attach a large screen monitor to it when you are at home. Having a comfortable environment for you to work in is critical to your success. You will also need periodic access to a printer to print out materials to help you train for your coding exercises. You may find that you can do without this if you are comfortable reading long articles on screen. However, many people find that they prefer printed material over reading material on the screen. The choice is really up to you.

The next item you need to consider is what software you will need. You will need a base operating system to run on software development tools, office automation software and backup software. The choice will depend on the programming language you decide to develop on. I will cover this in more detail in the upcoming material. The last item you will need is some basic home networking equipment. You will need access to the Internet and if you decide to have a notebook computer as your computer of choice, you will also need a wireless connection to make your development environment portable. Fortunately, home wireless connections are very affordable now and easy to come by.

Next, you will need to decide on your preferred programming language. Some of the most common choices for programming languages are Java from Oracle, the .NET platform from Microsoft, or the LAMP platform which is really Linux MySQL and PHP. If you are going to develop for the Java platform, you can either utilize the Windows operating system or Linux. If you decide to develop with Microsoft .NET you really have no choice but to develop on the Windows platform. Also if you decide to develop for the LAMP platform you really need to run Linux on your development computer. Another consideration is to decide if you are going to develop web-based applications, software for mobile applications or desktop software. If you decide you are going to develop mobile applications, you will probably need several physical devices to test your software on. Although you can use emulators for this, it is best to run final tests on actual physical hardware to make sure they work without any issues.

Here are some pitfalls to avoid when you are building your development environment. I cannot emphasize enough that you need to get the fastest computer you can possibly afford to develop code on.   Developing on old hardware and software will only lead to frustration to present a huge hurdle for you to overcome.   Most of the software vendors now have free development tools that you can download from the Internet. Examples of this are Microsoft Visual Studio community edition, the Eclipse environment for Java development and tools for Linux LAMP development. I will include links on how to get these tools as an attachment to this book.

As far as the hardware necessary for a typical .NET environment you will need a PC with a minimum of an i5 processor, although an i7 processor or equivalent is preferred.   You will need a minimum of 8 GB of RAM, although 16 would be better if you can afford it. Windows 10 is the current operating system and is probably the best environment for current .NET development although you could also use Windows server 2012 if you are using the cloud for your development environment. You should also get a 1 TB hard drive for installing software such as Visual Studio Community Edition 2015, Microsoft SQL Server Express, and you can also use Visual Studio Team Services for source control.

For a typical Java development environment, you have a choice of using either a PC or a Mac either one of these should at least have an i5 processor or better. You will also need 8 gigabytes of RAM on your computer although once again 16 would be better if you can afford it. After getting your PC you can download and install Eclipse for free as well as the MySQL database from Oracle. You can also use Visual Studio Team services for source control even though it is a Microsoft product. It is also a free web-based product.

For the LAMP environment, you can probably get by with a little bit less processor since the Linux operating system is very lightweight in terms of resources. There are many varieties of the Linux operating system such as Ubuntu, Red Hat, and others. You will have to decide which one is the best for you.

Your last consideration for your development environment is to consider building your development environment in the cloud. Microsoft Azure and Amazon AWS both offer very reasonable hosting fees to build your development server on. You can build a very fast machine and only pay for the server when it is running. By doing this you can build a much faster machine in the cloud and simply turn it off when you're not using it. Both Microsoft and Amazon offer free packages to get started, however, these machines are not typically fast enough to run software development tools. Another advantage of developing cloud-based servers is the Internet connection to these machines is extremely fast and downloading and installing software is significantly faster in the cloud than on your home computer. I am currently doing this and I found my productivity has increased significantly. Another advantage of doing this you will not have to invest in a fast computer, simply rent the time on the cloud and pay for what you use. I highly recommend you do this. If you do this, make sure to turn the computer off when you are not using it as these vendors charge by the minute for running the computer. I am currently spending about $20-$30 a month to run my development server on Amazon AWS.

In summary, just a final few tips for you as you build your development environment. First one is to try to find the fastest hardware you can afford as these development tools use a lot of resources and you will be frustrated with the slow environment if you do not get a fast computer. I also highly recommend that you look to cloud alternatives to lower your costs and increase your computer power. Also, make sure to keep your software tools up to the latest versions. This again will help minimize problems that you will encounter during your training. Another tip is to utilize source code control such as Git so you can store the code as you are practicing along the way. You can also use such tools as the Visual Studio Team Services, Codeplex, or DropBox to store your source code. After investing a lot of time writing code you will not want to lose it by not having it backed up in a proper location. This concludes this chapter. I hope I have given you some good information on building your development environment.

Exercise 2 Decide on Your Equipment

For this exercise, you will spec out your hardware for your development environment that you will need to train on. I have included some examples that you can use as a guideline when putting your own environment together.

Sample .NET Environment

- Hardware – Desktop
  - http://www.bestbuy.com/site/hp-envy-desktop-intel-core-i7-16gb-memory-2tb-hard-drive-brushed-aluminum/4370600.p?id=121973878 3376&skuId=4370600 $899.99
  - 25 Inch Monitor (an additional $299.99) quoted from Best Buy
- Software
  - Windows 10 Operating System (Included)
  - Visual Studio 2014 Community Edition Free
  - https://www.visualstudio.com/en-us/products/visual-studio-community-vs.aspx
  - Microsoft SQL Server 2016 Express Free
  - https://www.microsoft.com/en-us/download/details.aspx?id=52679

- Visual Studio Team Services Free
- https://www.visualstudio.com/en-us/products/visual-studio-team-services-vs.aspx

Sample .NET Development Environment (Cloud Based)

- Hardware –Amazon Windows 2012 Cloud Based Server
  - M4 Xtra Large 16 GB RAM 4 CPU 0.491/hour
  - Running this server 80 hours/month = 80*0.491 = $ 39.28 (storage will be an additional cost)
  - Source: https://aws.amazon.com/ec2/pricing/?sc_channel=PS&sc_campaign=acquisition_US&sc_publisher=google&sc_medium=ec2_b&sc_content=sitelink&sc_detail=aws%20server&sc_category=ec2&sc_segment=pricing&sc_matchtype=p&sc_country=US&s_kwcid=AL!4422!3!73821513642!p!!g!!aws%20server&ef_id=V5WBIQAABSqh4Eji:20160803014836:s
- Software
  - Windows 10 Operating System (Included)
  - Visual Studio 2014 Community Edition FREE
  - https://www.visualstudio.com/en-us/products/visual-studio-community-vs.aspx
  - Microsoft SQL Server 2016 Express

FREE
- https://www.microsoft.com/en-us/download/details.aspx?id=52679
- Visual Studio Team Services FREE
- https://www.visualstudio.com/en-us/products/visual-studio-team-services-vs.aspx

Sample Java Environment

- Notebook Computer – High End
    - http://www.dell.com/us/business/p/xps-13-9350-laptop-ubuntu/pd?oc=cax13ubuntus2102&model_id=xps-13-9350-laptop-ubuntu&l=en&s=bsd $2349.99 (quoted from Dell)
- Software
    - Current Java SDK FREE
    - http://www.oracle.com/technetwork/java/javase/downloads/index.html
    - Eclipse Enterprise Edition FREE
    - https://eclipse.org/downloads/
    - MySQL Database FREE
    - https://www.mysql.com/downloads/

Additional Information

- Best Laptop, Tablet & Desktop For Programming and Coding
    - http://www.triobest.com/best-laptop-for-programming-and-coding-for-

developers/

What Concepts Do I Need to Master?

Coding

Requirements

Concepts

Debugging

Testing

In this chapter, I will talk about the concepts that you need to master in order to become a successful programmer.

In order to become a successful programmer, to be able to produce working code and to contribute to software development projects, there are a number of concepts that you need to master. There are a number of fundamental concepts that are core to developing software. There are eight key concepts. These include requirements analysis, knowledge of database management systems, and HTML for web development. Also included on the list are basic networking concepts, software testing, and knowledge of the software development life cycle or SDLC. The last two items on the list are object oriented programming and detailed knowledge of your particular programming languages of choice such as C#, Java or PHP. There are certainly other concepts and they can be included depending on your career track, but this list represents the core of a foundational starting point. In the next material, I will go through each one of these in more detail.

Requirements Analysis

Requirements analysis is a great place to start. With requirements analysis, you are recording exactly the features that the customer desires in your software product. This can be difficult to do because often times customers do not know exactly what they want. An experienced programmer can help customers determine their exact requirements and lead to a successful project. This can be done through such techniques such as use cases, mockups, prototypes and user stories.

Database Management

Many systems today are web-based systems. Much of the data behind these web based systems is stored in a database and much of the code is devoted to interacting with the database from the website. In order to effectively design these programs, you need to have a command of fundamental database concepts. These include database design, normalization, and SQL or structured query language syntax for select statements, insert statements, update statements and delete statements. You will also need to master some type of programmatic access to the database from your programming language of choice. These include such technologies as ADO .NET, the Entity Framework, and Java database connectivity or JDBC. In order to effectively write codes, you will also need to master basic administration skills for a database. This will allow you to create new databases, back them up and restore them.

HTML

Another fundamental concept the programmers need to master is HTML or hypertext markup language. HTML is the basic building block of all web-based systems in production today. Skills that you will need to master are the basic syntax of HTML, design page layouts with HTML, and the document object model or DOM. You also need to understand such concepts as field validation and integrating JavaScript into your HTML code. Most programmers today also frequently use JavaScript libraries such as the JQuery library. This is also a necessary skill.

Networking

Most of the today's software products either interface with the Internet or a local area network. This means that programmers need to have a basic understanding of how networks function. You will need to understand how to interact with servers on a local area network or a wide area network. You also need to understand HTML protocols and how they interact over the Internet. Also, you need to be familiar with the IP addressing scheme used on the Internet as well as the domain name service or DNS. Another aspect of networking that you will need to be familiar with is how mobile devices interact with networks and their ability to be periodically connected to a network. This results in special techniques that mobile devices need to be able to connect to the Internet. This capability is called store and forward and is a very common need for these types of devices.

Testing

One of the most common areas that are overlooked in software developer training is the area of software testing. Even though this area is often overlooked, it is one of the most important activities in a software development project. Delivering quality software that is reliable is a primary goal of almost every software development project. Programmers need to understand such concepts as unit testing, functional testing, integration testing, and user acceptance testing or UAT. Without an effective software testing function, it is impossible to deliver quality working code.

Software Develpoment Lifecycle

The next area to understand is that of the software development lifecycle. The SDLC defines the process that software development teams use to produce working code. There are many different process models that software development teams use. Some of the more common methods are the agile methodology, the Scrum methodology, and waterfall development. Many companies will use their own proprietary model to develop softwares that are generally based on one of the methods mentioned above. Programmers must be familiar with these processes in order to be effective in a software development project. These processes define what programmers do on a daily basis in their job.

Object Oriented Programming

Most of the today's programming languages are based on an object-oriented model. Because of this, programmers need to be familiar with object oriented programming and design concepts. Including such common concepts as objects and classes, inheritance, polymorphism, and encapsulation.

Programming Language

The last but not least area that programmers need to be familiar with is their programming language of choice. You will need to understand the syntax of your chosen language such as Java or C# and be able to translate requirements into working code based on the syntax of your language. This will require quite a bit of practice to master the syntax of the language of choice.

In summary, there are a number of key concepts that a programmer needs to master. This may sound like an overwhelming list, but if you are able to master these concepts you will be able to function as an effective programmer. This will allow you to meet customer expectations in terms of delivering the required features of the software, building the software on time, and building it on a budget. In the next few lessons, I will lay out where you can get the training to master these concepts in how you can practice these for required certification tests. This concludes this chapter on concepts, I hope it gives you an idea of the concepts that you will need to master in order to become a good programmer.

Where Can I Get the Training?

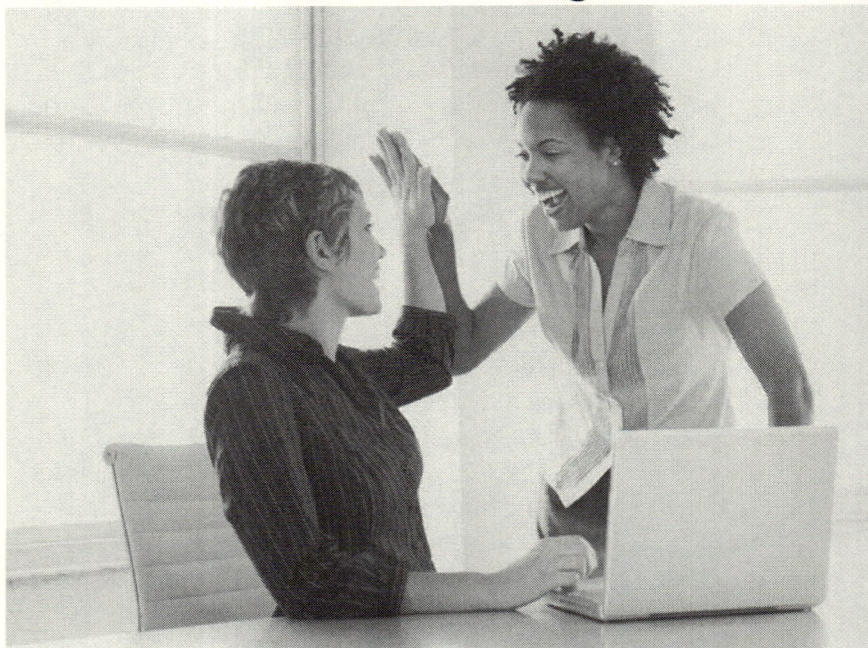

In this chapter, I will discuss the options for getting training to become a programmer. There are several options available today and each of these have advantages and disadvantages. So let's get started.

Training today can come from multiple sources. These include such sources as books, instructor-led classes, online classes, vendor product demonstrations, and mentorships. I will discuss each one of these in more detail.

Buying books and/or reading books online are one of the traditional ways of learning and is a great way to get started on the topic. Books are not nearly as expensive as instructor-led training and many books include a web-based format that is downloadable.

Books sometimes include companion websites with downloadable content such as tips and sample projects. There are also used books which are significantly less expensive than the new books. The major downside of books is that many people find them boring and many people prefer web-based video training classes that are popular today. I have found that a mixture of several different training methods works best for me.

Instructor-led classes are probably the most expensive option but is a time-tested way of learning. Many cities around the world offer Boot Camp types of classes that are very short and very focused on delivering software development skills. Some of these programs will even guarantee that you were able to be placed in a job after completing the training. These programs tend to be very expensive and you need to be careful about researching the program before you commit funds. You will want to research the reviews of these types of programs online and also consult with the Better Business Bureau if possible to determine the credibility of the programs. Another inexpensive way to get started with instructor-led classes is that you may want to look for Adult Education classes that are taught as continuing education. These classes tend to be significantly cheaper than traditional college classes and are a great way to get started.

Another method to get training is for the use of online classes. There are literally hundreds of sources that are available on the Internet that offer online classes. Options range from single classes to subscription-based models. The major disadvantage of these types of classes are you often do not have direct access to the instructor to help you with labs and programming practice. The other limitation of these classes is it is up to you to implement the coding exercises on your own computer without any help from an instructor. This can be overwhelming sometimes for a new student and causes them to become very frustrated. If you can find a mix of both on-premise classes and online classes, this will probably be the best option to give you both an affordable option with online classes and hands-on training with on-premise classes.

The last option to consider after you have completed your initial training is a mentorship program. These programs are somewhat difficult to find and you generally have to be selected from a pool of applicants, Many programs will pay you as you are an apprentice in the program and you can learn to code from a senior developer. I have included some examples of these types of programs as links in the supporting document to this lecture. This approach is generally much better to take after you have already completed some initial training.

The last area I will talk about is getting training through vendor product demonstrations. Many vendors hold free product training sessions throughout the country. Vendors such as Microsoft and Oracle regularly provide training on their latest software development tools and techniques. This is also a great way to keep up with new development techniques that are being offered by various vendors.

In the previous material, I have outlined several different types of training sources. Each of them has advantages and disadvantages and you will need to consider these as you develop your plan and budget. Developing this plan and budget is an exercise that I have included in this book. Your budget and your timetable will help shape the types of training that you can afford in terms of time and money. The sample training plans that I have included will also help you decide which training is best. This concludes this chapter I hope it has given you some good ideas for training that you can include in your plan.

Entry Level Certifications

This chapter I will talk about entry-level certifications that are available for programmers. These certifications are available from a number of different vendors and it will depend on the technology track that you have chosen for your training. Let's talk about some of the details of each of these.

Since you will be applying for a job without a formal degree, certification will become more important. The certifications will indicate to an employer that you have proven the basic skills with a particular product or developmental tool. These products and certifications change over time so it is important to keep up with updates these products change. Next, I will talk about basic certification for Microsoft .Net, Oracle's Java, PHP, and some other types of certifications.

The first area of certification I will talk about is for Microsoft.Net and their Microsoft Certified Solutions Developer certification. In order to obtain this certification, you will need to pass three exams. These are programming in HTML5 with JavaScript, Developing with ASP .NET MVC, and developing with Microsoft Azure. You can find out more information about .NET certification from the Microsoft website: https://www.microsoft.com/en-us/learning/certification-overview.aspx

The next area I have included some information about is Java certification. The entry level Java certification is called Java Foundations Certified Junior Developer Associate.   You can find more information about this certification here in the Oracle web site: https://education.oracle.com

PHP also has several certifications that you can obtain. These include the certificate from the W3C school which includes MySQL and also the Zend PHP certification.

There are also other certifications that you can pursue as well. These include certifications for cloud-based operations such as Salesforce.com, Microsoft Azure, Amazon AWS, and several mobile certifications.

In summary, entry-level certifications exist for all the major platforms. The certifications are very helpful when you do not have a degree or much experience and you are looking for your first job. Many of the certifications have the low-cost web-based training to help you study for the exam. Certification needs to be combined with hands-on experience to be the most effective. Some of these exams can even be taken over the Internet. This concludes this chapter on certification. I hope it has given you a good starting point for planning certifications on your master training plan.

Exercise 3 Complete Your Training Plan

In this exercise, you will write up your own training plan and lay out the details of what classes you will take and/or any certifications you will get as well. I have included some samples that you can model your own plan against. I did not include prices for these classes since they change frequently for online classes. Also, I am not recommending any of these classes. You should check the reviews and make your own decision.

Sample .NET Training Plan

- Udemy Classes
- Requirements Class
  - https://www.udemy.com/software-requirements-gathering/
  - C# Class
  - https://www.udemy.com/programming-for-complete-beginners-in-csharp/
- ASP .NET Class
  - https://www.udemy.com/the-complete-aspnet-mvc-5-course/
- Database Class
  - https://www.udemy.com/csharpbasics/
- HTML 5 Class
  - https://www.udemy.com/complete-html5-and-css3-course-1-start-to-finish-project/

- Software Testing Class
    - https://www.udemy.com/qa-software-testing-training-course/
- SDLC Class
    - https://www.udemy.com/the-agile-samurai-bootcamp/

Sample Java Training Plan

Udemy Classes:
- Requirements Class
  - https://www.udemy.com/software-requirements-gathering
- Java Class
  - https://www.udemy.com/learn-java-programming-from-scratch/
- Java Server Pages Class
  - https://www.udemy.com/jsp-tutorial
- Database Class
  - https://www.udemy.com/csharpbasics
- HTML 5 Class
  - https://www.udemy.com/complete-html5-and-css3-course-1-start-to-finish-project
- Software Testing Class
  - https://www.udemy.com/qa-software-testing-training-course
- SDLC Class
  - https://www.udemy.com/the-agile-samurai-bootcamp

Sample Developer Bootcamps

Online bootcamp finder:

https://www.thinkful.com/bootcamps/all/

- Bootcamp Sample #1
    - TechElevator http://www.techelevator.com/
    - Located in Cleveland Ohio
    - Basic Cost $12,000 (please check their website for current information)
    - Program 14 Weeks

- Bootcamp Sample #2
    - FlatIron School https://flatironschool.com/
    - Located in NC
    - Basic Cost $15,000 (please check their website for current information)
    - Program Length 12 Weeks

Writing Your Resume

In this chapter, will talk about writing your resume. I will give you some tips on writing your resume and what information is useful to include. So let's get started.

Your resume is the first thing that an HR department or an employer will see from you. You will want to make a good first impression. It is important that you give this document a professional appearance. You might want to consider getting help online or from a recruiter that is often times happy to help you. Since you are applying to become a software developer you will need to highlight specific languages and platforms you have worked on. This might be difficult since this is your first job you are applying for, but you can highlight languages and platforms that you have worked on during your training experience. Project experience is also very important. Since this is your first job you should be able to include projects you have worked on in a classroom setting and perhaps a project that you have volunteered for. Any type of project experience is important because it tells the hiring managers the kinds of things that you had access to while you were training. You should be able to find online templates from Microsoft and Google for resumes. I have included links for some of these that I found in the next exercise in this book. One of the other things you might consider is constructing a web-based resume. WIX offers a free service for this. Another tip is, LinkedIn can export your profile as a PDF file in this can be useful as a resume as well.

Some other useful tips for your resume are the following. Since this is an entry-level position keep your resume to one page if possible. Once you have more experience it is acceptable to have a longer resume that highlights your project experience. Be sure to include all the relevant contact information in your resume. This should include your email address, cell phone number, LinkedIn account, a link to your online resume if you have one. Any links to any sample projects if you have them are also important.

In summary, with a little work and research, you can make your resume really stand out and look very professional. This concludes this chapter on resumes I hope it helps.

Exercise 4 Write Your Resume

In this exercise, you will write you will write your own resume. I have included some resources that will help you with this. Do not over think this process. Many people stress over this process. You simply need to follow some good examples and include your own information.

- Sample Programmer Resume from Monster.com
    - http://www.monster.com/career-advice/article/sample-resume-computer-programmer-entry-level
    - http://www.resume-resource.com/computer-programmer-resume-example/
- Resume Template from Monster
    - View and download the Entry-Level Computer Programmer resume template in Word.
- Resume Checking Sites
    - https://www.livecareer.com/resume-check?utm_source=google&utm_medium=cpc&gclid=CPy4xeaapM4CFVYbgQodrAIOrw

Get Some Experience First

In order to get your first job, most companies will want some prior programming experience first. This seems crazy since it is your very first programming job. Fortunately, there are some things you can do to help this.

One of the easiest things you can do is to volunteer to help with a non-profit organization such as a church or club that needs some IT project help. This can be a good deal for both of you. You can get some real world experience to put on a resume and the organization can get some help with their projects. Many of these tasks will not be hard code development projects but will be tasks like helping to build a website or publishing newsletters. You can be a resource for these organizations to help get things done.

Another way to get some experience is to develop a simple mobile app and publish it to the App Store for iPhone or Google Play. This is a more difficult and will take some time, but you can point to a real world piece of software that you created. This app does not need to be complex but does need to be functional. This is a great thing to include on your resume.

In addition to writing a mobile app, you can also write simple websites and deployed it on the free trial of Amazon AWS or Microsoft Azure. These apps are publicly visible over the Internet and can be demonstrated to potential employers.

With a bit of hard work and imagination, you can create opportunities to showcase your experience. You do not need a paying job to get your very first software development experience.

Interview Tips

After you complete your training you will want to get ready to go on a number of interviews to get your first job. In this lesson, I will go over a number of interview tips that can help you out during this process. So let's get started.

The following tips are based on my experience in both giving interviews and being interviewed over a number of years. This process can be very nerve-racking especially when you are going through it for the first time. The only way to get better at this process is through practice. After you have been interviewed a number of times, you will become much more comfortable with the process.

My number one tip to have a successful interview is to show up early. Being late for an interview is a disaster. No matter what your excuse is, it's almost impossible to overcome being late to a job interview. This makes a very bad impression on employers. In addition, you will feel rushed and you will not be able to perform at your best. If you show up early and are able to sit and focus before your interview, it will give you time to relax before you begin the interview process. Also by showing up early it shows employers that you are conscientious and you are able to keep your commitments.

Another thing you have to overcome with an interview is nervousness. It is very natural to be nervous for an interview and I have found out that if you are very nervous it's better to just tell the interviewer that you are. It will help you relax during the process. If you go ahead and admit that you are nervous it allows the employer to see a very honest and the open side of you. Again being nervous can be overcome through practice.

My next tip is to be very honest when answering questions. If you don't know the answer just say so. Faking it in the technical interview is very bad. Most technical hiring managers know when somebody is making up an answer and it leaves a very bad impression. Simply not knowing the answer is not necessarily bad and you could just tell them you have not been exposed to that particular concept or if you do know something similar perhaps you can expand on that but just admit when you don't know something it's far better.

Before your interview, you should research the company you are interviewing with. It leaves a very good impression if you know something about the company and you have done your homework before hand. It shows the company that you have initiative and are willing to go the extra mile to get things done.

Once you begin your interview questions one good thing to remember is software development is a team effort. Make sure you come across as a team player. Most software development shops employ quite a few people. Working as a good team member is a critical skill. If you can be sure and mention any other jobs you have worked in that reflects your team skills.

Many recruiters will tell you to wear a suit and tie or formal business attire to the interview. Most software shops today are not that formal and it is probably more appropriate for an entry-level programmer to dress business casual. I will leave that up to you.

Another nice touch for an interview is to follow up with the written card to thank them for their time. This may sound strange, but it will leave a good impression. Mention in the thank you letter how you feel your skillset and team work would be a good fit for the company.

My last tip is to try to be yourself and have fun with the process. Once again I want to emphasize this process will get easier over time. I have added some sample interview questions in the next chapter and many of them are non-technical questions. These non-technical questions are very important to hiring managers so please do not ignore them. I hope I have given you some good tips to prepare you for your interview and good luck with the process.

Where to Look for Jobs

MONSTER

In this chapter, I will go through some tips on where to look for jobs. We will look at some several different sources that you can look for jobs and how you can best communicate to potential employers. So let's go ahead and get started.

When you first start looking for a job there is a ton of information on the Internet, but it is a bit overwhelming for a first-time job seeker. We will review four different places that offers different opportunities for job seekers. Let's got through each one of these in detail.

Linkedin

The first site that I will cover is LinkedIn. LinkedIn is a great way to build your professional network. Recently they have also added job postings to this site as well and it is a very active place for potential employers. Start by filling up your profile and make sure it is complete. Next you can start building your network by including professional references people you work with and job recruiters as. Not only is the site useful for finding your first job but it may be very useful in finding other opportunities throughout your career. LinkedIn also has the capability of exporting your profile to a PDF file and can be used as a resume as well.

Monster.com

Monster is one of the major job posting sites and there are many others like monster as well. Monster will be able to help you target jobs by classification as well as by geographic area. A lot of information will be generated from the site for you but you need to make sure to keep up with email and phone calls from job leads.

Craigslist

One often overlooked site for jobs is Craigslist. This site typically only posts entry-level jobs, but it may be a great way to get started with a help desk position or a support position. After that you will be able to work your way up.

Recruiting Services

Another way to look for jobs is for the use of a recruiting service. Check the local ads to see what services are available in your area. You can also check with your friends and family to see if they have any recommendations. If you are attending a programming Boot Camp, check with your instructor to see which service they might recommend.

In summary, you need to have multiple sources to be able to get the right job. Keep a log of all the places you have contacted and all the people you have talked to so that you will not get confused when they call you back. You may need to start with a support position and work your way up to a programming position. Try to enjoy this process even though it might be frustrating after getting your first job do not worry things will get much easier. Good luck on your job search!

Exercise 5 Write Your Job Search Plan

The following is a sample of a simple job search plan. You should develop you own plan and checklist to keep your job search on track. You should also assign dates where ever possible to help make sure your plan stays on time wherever possible and keeps you motivated.

- Step 1 Build Complete profile on LinkedIn http://www.linkedin.com
  - o Check listing in local area on linked in
  - o Also, check for listing for remote work as well
- Step 2 Build a profile on Monster.com http://www.monster.com/
  - o Check listing in local area
  - o Checklists for local companies and see if you know anyone at those companies that are hiring
- Step 3 Build your online resume on WIX http://www.wix.com/
- Step 4 Look through your email contact to see who might be able to help you with your job search
- Step 5 Contact local recruiting companies so they can begin to help you in your search, select one to start with
- Step 6 begin preparing for your interviews

Interview Questions

In this chapter, I have collected a number of interview questions that I have either been given in an interview or I have asked candidates myself. Over my career, I have interviewed hundreds of programmers and I have included my tips on what hiring managers are looking for in responses to each of the questions. To make things a bit easier I have grouped these sample questions in a number of areas. You should expect to get questions from each of these areas in your interview.

General Background Questions

- Tell us about your background?
- Describe you background with software development.
- Describe your experience with C# development. (or whatever language the job requires)
- Describe your experience with developing web-based systems?

General Technical Questions

- Describe a code review and why a code review is a required part of the development process?
- Explain Service Oriented Architecture (SOA)? How does SOA differ from a Web Service? What factors will you consider when utilizing Web Services?

Detailed Technical Questions

- What is a stored procedure and what are some of the advantages of using one?
- What is an Object? What is a Class? What is the difference between the two?
- What are some of the recommended best practices to optimize stored procedure performance?
- Explain why you would standardize exception handling for multiple tiered .NET applications on an enterprise-wide basis?
- What does GAC stand for and how is it used? What are some of the requirements for use of the GAC?

Work Style and Team Work

- What was you most successful project and why was that project successful?
- How do you manage time and manage priorities to meet critical deadlines?

Book Summary

Thank you so much for reading this book. If you have questions or comments, please send them to sales@destinlearning.com and I will get back to you as quickly as possible. I will add more material and resources to YouTube and the Destin Learning website. So please look for updates as I will periodically post new materials. Again thank you so much and good luck in your new career!

About the Author

Eric Frick

I have been involved in software development and IT operations for 30 years. I have worked as a Software Developer, Software Development Manager, Software Architect and as an Operations Manager. In addition, for the last five years have I taught evening classes on various IT related subjects at several local universities. In 2015 I founded destinlearning.com and I am developing a series of online classes and books that can provide practical information to students on various IT and software development topics.

More From Destin Learning

YouTube

Thank you so much for your interest in this book. I hope it has given you a good start in the exciting field of Information Technology. You can see more from my YouTube channel where I am continuing to post free videos about software development. If you subscribe to my channel you will get updates as I post new material weekly:

http://youtube.com/destinlearning

You can also sign up for my newsletter at http://destinlearning.com where I will send out updates on new material. Thank you again and good luck with your future with Information Technology!

Appendix A YouTube Videos

In addition to this book I have also published a number of these lessons as YouTube Videos.   Listed below are the links to these videos. You can subscribe to my YouTube channel at:

http://youtube.com/destinlearning

49995650R00045

Made in the USA
Columbia, SC
30 January 2019